THE ULTIMATE GUIDE TO
BEER COCKTAILS

—•≫≪•—

THE ULTIMATE GUIDE TO
BEER COCKTAILS

—•≫≪•—

50 CREATIVE RECIPES FOR COMBINING BEER AND BOOZE

JON *AND* LINDSAY YEAGER
FOUNDERS OF POURTASTE

Skyhorse Publishing

Skyhorse Publishing books may be purchased in bulk at special discounts for sales promotion, corporate gifts, fund-raising, or educational purposes. Special editions can also be created to specifications. For details, contact the Special Sales Department, Skyhorse Publishing, 307 West 36th Street, 11th Floor, New York, NY 10018 or info@skyhorsepublishing.com.

Skyhorse® and Skyhorse Publishing® are registered trademarks of Skyhorse Publishing, Inc.®, a Delaware corporation.

Visit our website at www.skyhorsepublishing.com.

10 9 8 7 6 5 4 3 2 1

Library of Congress Cataloging-in-Publication Data is available on file.

Cover design by Mona Lin
Cover photograph by Laurie Dicus

Print ISBN: 978-1-5107-2921-6
Ebook ISBN: 978-1-5107-2925-4

Printed in China

Contents

Introduction

Beer-cocktails. Sounds a little funny, right? What many bartenders across the globe are trying to perfect is still a little foreign to most imbibers. Many people know the joys, and the woes, of the venerable Margarona, or Coronita, or Beergarita, depending on where you're from. It's the classic Margarita with a Corona injected right into the middle. Whether frozen or on the rocks, the upside-down glass bottle rising from what is often a much too sweet cocktail is a simple man's pleasure. It's available at basically every Mexican restaurant and it definitely does the trick.

Beyond that though, the marriage of brew and booze is a path less traveled. The tastemakers of today's craft cocktail community take this offshoot of cocktail history pretty seriously, and we've tasted a number of wonderful beer cocktails in our travels. The problem is, that beyond the cocktail elite, this art form of spirits and suds isn't experimented with much and we think that should change. We hope this book can be an inspiration to flavor and technique. Considering this beverage genre has basically no boundaries, we hope that these recipes might serve as a resource to think outside the box the next time you go shake something up. We don't know much, and there's been much trial and error, but as full-time consultants, we hope to share some of our successes with you. Hopefully, this book can open a door for you into how we interpret what a cocktail can be. To make sure we're speaking the same language though, a brief history . . .

History

BEER

The marriage of beer and other ingredients has a long history—longer than one might expect. For example, there was the discovery of what could be the first paycheck from 5,000 BC. Found in the ancient city of Uruk (in today's Iraq), we see an inscription in which a laborer was compensated with fermented beverages depending on his day's work. We can't judge, we have those days, too.

Then there's the Code of Hammurabi. Hammurabi was the sixth king of Babylon and, as it stands, sort of led the way for the idea of governing law and having something like a constitution in place. In this code, which was chiseled in stone much like the Ten Commandments, we see all the makings of a well-oiled civilization. There are laws for landowners, violence, theft, and even laws for divorce. But, this hand-carved set of rules also dealt with the growing and harvesting of grain for the sake of beverages. Further, there are laws on the beverages' sales and distribution. Through this code, historians have put together that these ancient Babylonians had beer halls, run by women (as there were probably other activities happening behind closed doors), and these women had a pretty strict time running these businesses. The downside was if they slipped up, they'd be burned at the stake or drowned.

The upside? Most possibly the advent of the local bar, and we all know that's good news. Through all this though, there's one document in particular that sticks out. Though we have evidence of humans producing alcohol and how important that alcohol was to them and their economy, this document not only spells out the recipe but really starts to peek inside the culinary mindset of the day. The story goes that ancient Sumerians had a goddess of brewing named Ninkasi. Some fella, or lady, wrote a poem to the goddess which documented the process in which they produced this yet-to-be-defined beverage. Coming to us on two clay tablets from 1800 BC, the Hymn of Ninkasi stands as the first archeological evidence for a barley-based beer. And though this is the style we are used to today, the use of ingredients outside traditional grains, water, and yeast are inspiring for the cocktail-minded.

The poem was translated out of the University of Chicago and put into the hands of Fritz Maytag, founder of Anchor Brewing in San Francisco. They replicated the recipe from the direct translation and presented their results at the annual meeting of the American Association of Microbrews in 1991. Miguel Civil, the leading translator, wrote, "we were able to taste 'Ninkasi Beer,' sipping it from large jugs with drinking straws as they did four millennia ago. The beer had an alcohol concentration of 3.5%, very similar to modern beers, and had a 'dry taste lacking in bitterness,' similar to hard apple cider." The first part of the longer poem reads as follows:

Borne of the flowing water,
Tenderly cared for by the Ninhursag,
Borne of the flowing water,
Tenderly cared for by the Ninhursag,
Having founded your town by the sacred lake,
She finished its great walls for you,
Ninkasi, having founded your town by the sacred lake,
She finished its walls for you,
Your father is Enki, Lord Nidimmud,

Your mother is Ninti, the queen of the sacred lake.

Ninkasi, your father is Enki, Lord Nidimmud,

Your mother is Ninti, the queen of the sacred lake.

You are the one who handles the dough [and] with a big shovel,

Mixing in a pit, the bappir with sweet aromatics,

Ninkasi, you are the one who handles the dough [and] with a big shovel,

Mixing in a pit, the bappir with [date] honey,

You are the one who bakes the bappir in the big oven,

Puts in order the piles of hulled grains,

Ninkasi, you are the one who bakes the bappir in the big oven,

Puts in order the piles of hulled grains,

You are the one who waters the malt set on the ground,

The noble dogs keep away even the potentates,

Ninkasi, you are the one who waters the malt set on the ground,

The noble dogs keep away even the potentates,

You are the one who soaks the malt in a jar,

The waves rise, the waves fall.

Ninkasi, you are the one who soaks the malt in a jar,

The waves rise, the waves fall.

You are the one who spreads the cooked mash on large reed mats,

Coolness overcomes,

Ninkasi, you are the one who spreads the cooked mash on large reed mats,

Coolness overcomes,

You are the one who holds with both hands the great sweet wort,

Brewing [it] with honey [and] wine
(You the sweet wort to the vessel)
Ninkasi, (. . .)(You the sweet wort to the vessel)
The filtering vat, which makes a pleasant sound,
You place appropriately on a large collector vat.
Ninkasi, the filtering vat, which makes a pleasant sound,
You place appropriately on a large collector vat.
When you pour out the filtered beer of the collector vat,
It is [like] the onrush of Tigris and Euphrates.
Ninkasi, you are the one who pours out the filtered beer of the collector vat,
It is [like] the onrush of Tigris and Euphrates.

As a cocktail geek, a few things stick out. First, the use of dates and honey in this recipe. Beer is largely based of grains. But having the other ingredients (were there other "sweet aromatics"?) adds complexity and gives us cocktail fans some other flavors to grab onto. Second, the beverage was consumed through straws. Now, I will never drink my beer through a straw, but it's interesting. This tells me a little more about mouth feel, weight, and so on. For those budding mixologists, what about this: combine honey, cream sherry (which has overt date and fig nuances), and lemon juice, for balance. Shake this in equal proportions, strain neat into a cocktail glass, and top with a trusted lager or pilsner. Sounds like we're onto something, doesn't it?

Fast forward through history, to when Christ was walking, and we see the use of gruit. Gruit is an herb mixture used for bittering beer, prior to the discovery of hops. There might not seem to be a cocktail connection here but what the Holy Roman Empire realized was that in addition to ingredients such as mugwort, horehound, and yarrow, other spices like juniper berries, ginger and cinnamon also made for wonderful aromatics. The gradual transition from the use of gruit to hops, and its role in the Reformation, is a wonderful read, but as cocktail enthusiasts, we just can't get away from gruit. The aromatics and flavors used in the beers of the Middle Ages sound like an enticing cocktail to us.

Think about it this way: if juniper berry is the dominant flavor for gin (and it is for the London Dry style), then let's pair a few flavors like the Romans did. What about a gin-based cocktail with ginger (syrup or liqueur), a little lemon or lime juice for balance, and then top the sucker off with . . . say, a lambic-style raspberry beer, or sour style that often yields a lemon-like acidity. Sounds great, right!? As we hop, skip, and jump through history we then turn our attention to the Shandygaff, or Shandy. Finding its way into print in the middle of the nineteenth century, the Shandy, or new-fangled drink of the day, was originally a beer with either ginger beer or ginger ale. Lemon-lime soda also played a decent role in the Shandy's definition through the turn of the twentieth century until Germany's take on the matter, the Radler, comes into play. Just a quick offshoot of the Shandy, Germany began to experiment with grapefruit juice as the predominant citrus element. There's been some confusion on the actual difference between Radlers and Shandies. We say *toe-may-toe, toe-mah-toe*. Essentially these are referencing the same drink with minor differences, but the success of both the Shandy and Radler have caused brands to pre-bottle these, much to our delight.

COCKTAILS

Now that we've explored what it means to put a little something extra into beer, let's look at this from the other angle, the cocktail angle. What is it to make a full libation, only with a hint of beer as an additional component? Or further, using beer as the libation's base with multiple other ingredients? The spirit-driven "cocktail" has a long history, going all the way back to the early seventeenth century, with its roots being in the Punch traditions of London.

In the age of exploration, the British were often the dominating force, and they were exceptionally good at sea. They were so much at the top of their game that it was often said that "the sun never set on the British empire," as they were conquering all four corners of the globe. Their travels through the Indian Ocean, hitting Malaysia, Java, and other South Seas outposts, however, documented a large format concoction batched by the locals of spirit, sugar, water, citrus, and spice known as *paunch* (Hindi word for *five*). As word got back home of the native way to spend the evening (or afternoon, or morning for that matter), it quickly became adopted by high society. The art and act of punch-making, and its call to stop and relax, was to Industrial England what grabbing a cup of joe at a coffee shop is today (and those two were almost born out of the same place of English business).

The individualized cocktail, however, was purely an American innovation. As we broke away from the motherland through the American Revolution, the fads of yore were no longer acceptable. Plus, we were busy. Busy discovering our new land and our priorities as a young nation. It is here that Punch became smaller, quicker, and where much discovery happened as to what you could actually mix.

But where does beer play into all of this? The first reference we find for this is Purl. This seventeenth century creation made quite a name for itself in the creation of what we commonly refer to as *the cocktail*. Purl was bitter ale, infused with wormwood and other botanicals and was intended as a morning stomach soother. As basic as that sounds, the lifespan of this recipe has much to do with cocktail history. The Purl's grown-up, and wine-based cousin, the Purl Royale, is the first documentation we have about the addition of commercial bitters in a libation of any sort.

Further, the nineteenth century version is quite a bit more exotic. In Charles Dickens's *Our Mutual Friend*, we see a more sophisticated mixture of hot ale, gin, sugar, and eggs. Now that sounds a bit more like a modern cocktail, does it not? Fast forward to Civil War–era United States and the godfather of mixology, Jerry "The Professor" Thomas, was the first person to document the growing trade of mixed drinks into the first-ever recipe guide. Unlike this book, or any other like it, Thomas's guide was a trade manual for industry only. The 1862 title *How to Mix Drinks, or The Bon Vivant's Companion* defined for the first time a comprehensive list of the various styles of mixed drinks, which included cocktails, toddies, juleps, flips, smashes, and so on. By today's standards they're all "cocktails," but in Jerry's day not all alcoholic combinations flew by the same feather.

Interestingly enough, the use of beer in a mixed drink was pronounced enough in this era that the good professor himself thought it important to include a few beer-tails of his own. The Porter Cup happens to be one of my favorites. With Porter-style beer and ale as its base, the addition of brandy, ginger, and cucumber round this out to be a serious summer delight. Think about it as an effervescent Pimm's Cup! Or take for instance

Ale Punch, with mild ale, white wine, brandy, lemon, and capillaire, which is sort of a bitter orange syrup. As we progress into the twentieth century, the combination of beer and other ingredients becomes a bit more basic, and decidedly less documented. Beyond England's shandy-gaff and Germany's radler, the Margarona came along somewhere in our lifetime, as does the Michelada, Mexico's horse in the race that includes lime juice, salt, and an assortment of hot sauces or spices. At the end of it, beer and cocktails have been in close proximity to each other, it seems, the whole time.

Tools, Technique, and Other Tidbits

For those of you who aren't professional bartenders, constantly tinkering, creating, and perfecting, it might be helpful to have an overview of what's needed and things to consider when making not only our recipes, but yours as well.

The reason we **shake or stir** a cocktail is not only to make the drink cold, but more importantly, to dilute the cocktail to a balanced point. On a molecular level, we need water to break up alcohol compounds, which in turn releases aroma. Knowing that our nose and mouth are so connected, this "aroma release" can quickly change our perception of the actual flavor. On a more practical level, that bit of water we're introducing calms everything down. It makes any recipe something you can sip on for a bit and gives us the opportunity to safely have more than one. The *way* we dilute the drink, however, adds a certain weight to the drink or a "mouth feel." This is where shaking versus stirring comes in. Again, this might be old hat for some, but for the novice home bartender consider the following in your preparation. Shaking a drink introduces air to the recipe. The aeration that's happening in the shaking tin produces a lighter and more refreshing experience. Think of a well-made Margarita on the rocks, or a balanced Daiquiri. These drinks are light, fun, bright, etc.

On the reverse side, we have stirred drinks. Stirring keeps air *out* of the drink. This method still gets us the dilution and temperature we need but, with no air introduced, the body of the cocktail will be heavier. Think about well-made Manhattans or a true, historically accurate Martini. These drinks are like velvet on the tongue. They're mature sippers that have a little chest hair, if you will. We've spelled out which recipes you should shake and which you should stir in this book, but as you find yourself creating your own recipes (and you should) think about what's in the glass and how you should treat it. Recipes that contain fruit juices, anything muddled, like mint or cucumber, and even dairy and eggs, are shaken drinks. Libations that are spirit-driven can pretty much be assumed as stirred. I'm positive there's an exception somewhere, and I'm familiar with the crowd who swears by shaking straight vodka and calling it a day, but this one rule of thumb should get you by.

Ice is another big one for bartenders. The best of the best promote ice machines that produce solid cubes which account for the way the cocktail responds, be it shaken or stirred. These specialty cubes really do matter when prepping a cocktail, but at home we're not so lucky. Assuming we're all working with refrigerator-produced ice or something in a bag, brought to the party, it's important to pay attention to your drink via straw tasting. We bring up the ice subject to say this. The cheaper the ice, or the smaller the cube, the quicker the dilution. Nobody wants a watered-down cocktail, and this is prevented by tasting your drinks with a straw, directly from the shaking tin or mixing glass, before you serve it. Depending on the exact ice you're working with, start with a few shakes or just a few seconds of stirring in your mixing glass. Go longer if needed but it's better to start small. As a real-life example, we've used quickly melting gas station ice at events where our normal "shake and stir" time is cut in half because the ice just won't hold up. In those instances, we shake really hard, really fast (to get the drink chilled) and then once it's to taste we quickly get it off the ice. Tip: remember that once your liquids hit ice, no matter which kind, your time clock has started.

This book calls for **fruit zests** in many of the recipes. Oranges, lemons, and grapefruits have oils in the skin that, when expressed, add complexity to the top layer of a cocktail, or the nose. Though chefs might use a grater to allow small pieces of rind to fall into a dish, bartenders don't want those little floaties in your drink. A common vegetable peeler can yield a piece of zest about the size of a standard band-aid. Simply peel from the top of the fruit to the bottom for one piece of zest. To express the oil onto your drink, face the pigment side of the zest, or the side with color, towards your cocktail. Hovering about 2 inches above the drink, give the fruit a hard snap and you should see the oils release. You can discard the fruit or decoratively set it in the libation.

Finally, "**rinsing**." Rinsing is the act of coating the inside of your glass with a certain spirit for its aromatics only. Simply pour your rinsing spirit into the glass and roll it around with your hand to coat the entire inside of the glass.

The tools you'll need for these recipes, and basically any others, include:

- Shaking tin
- Mixing glass
- Barspoon
- Hawthorn strainer (the common type of strainer with a circled coil)
- Julep strainer (the large, slotted spoon that's more elegant with stirred drinks)
- Muddler
- Paring knife
- Cutting board
- Jigger (we suggest a 2:1 ratio—this will be sufficient no matter the recipe)

In this book, you might see a few ingredients that are unfamiliar. Here's a quick overview of boutique ingredients and verbiage:

AMARO: Amaro is an intentionally bitter Italian liqueur. The two main styles are dark amari (pl), which offer roasted spice, caramel, and sometimes cola-like flavors. The other main style, brighter and more vegetal, is a red bitter, with the most popular brand being Campari.

APPLEJACK: American-born apple brandy from Laird & Co. Known as America's oldest distillery, Laird's version is more similar to whiskey as opposed to the more fruit-forward apple brandy from France known as Calvados.

ARMAGNAC: A grape-based and barrel-aged brandy from France. Armagnac is the tougher, older brother to Cognac. We often say that Armagnac is to rye whiskey what Cognac is to Bourbon. Armagnac tends to add a little chest hair.

ARRACK: Most likely the oldest *distilled* spirit in the world. Arrack is a common Asian term for a distilled spirit, with various types being distilled from palm and coconut sap or sugar cane. This book calls for the sugar cane- and red rice-based Batavia Arrack specifically, which is the historically relevant version first used in the time of Punch.

BENEDICTINE: A French-born, herbal, monastic liqueur. True Benedictine is more potent than its more popular cousin B&B, which is diluted with brandy. Stick with the real stuff.

BONAL: French-born quinine and gentian liquor, offering bitterness to cocktails. We've found that Bonal can often soften the edges of other flavors and "round out" a recipe.

CACHACA: Un-aged Brazilian rum which is produced from the sugar cane juice, as opposed to the molasses. This difference yields a clear, exotic, and funky distillate. Cachaca is typically reserved for the classic Caipirinha, but bartenders lately are finding new and exciting ways to incorporate this rum.

CALVADOS: French apple brandy produced in the Normandy and Brittany areas. Some calvados will have some element of pear in their distillate as well.

CAPPELLETTI: A red, Italian bitter amaro similar to, but lighter than, Campari.

CHARTREUSE: A French-born, herbal liqueur. With the traditional green and a slightly sweeter yellow version available, these liqueurs offer crisp, alpine nuances to cocktails.

DRY CURACAO: As the same suggests, this specific ingredient is a drier, slightly bitter, and historically accurate orange liqueur, as used in the nineteenth century. This is opposed to the sweeter and thicker orange spirits like Grand Marnier or Cointreau.

EAU DU VIE: The literal translation means "water of life," and is not specific to any one category. But in today's cocktail circles, *eau du vie* generally refers to high-end fruit liqueurs and cordials. Creating a distinction between higher end cordials as *eau du vie* from the overly sweetened, not to mention fake, spirits has been profoundly needed through the cocktail renaissance. A good pepsi challenge is to taste a bottom shelf raspberry or peach liqueur next to something produced in Europe. You'll see what we're talking about.

FALERNUM: A pre-bottled island syrup typically based off ginger, lime, and almond. This tropical mixture can also contain other native spices such as cinnamon, allspice, star anise, and more, and is often bottled with a touch of rum for flavor and preservative qualities.

GRAPPA: Un-aged, Italian grape brandy made from the leftovers of wine production. In this book, we call for Nardini's Mandorla grappa, which includes an infusion of almonds and cherries. Grappa can often be a fierce spirit, but Nardini and a few others are making some beautiful brandies that are well-suited for cocktails.

JAGGERY: An unrefined version of sugar that is popular in Asia and Southeast Asia. Purchased in small blocks, the producers of this sugar do not separate the molasses, rather they keep all liquids together. It was this form of sugar that first made its way into Punch (see History/Cocktails on page xiv).

MEAD: Mead is fermented honey wine and is most likely the oldest alcoholic beverage in the world.

ORGEAT: Almond syrup that traditionally has orange blossom water or rose water included for depth.

PAMPLEMOUSSE: French-born grapefruit liquor.

PISCO: Un-aged South American grade brandy. Coming from either Peru or Chile, this spirit is earthy, sometimes a little musty and, blindly tasted, can be associated with a blanco tequila. Historically, pisco is reserved for classics like the Pisco Sour or San Francisco's Pisco Punch. The forward-thinking cocktail elite, however, have been thinking outside the box with this spirit for some time.

SWEDISH PUNSCH: A red rice and sugar cane distillate that was made to order in the nineteenth century prior to the bottled version we see today. It is a slightly sweet Nordic liqueur with spices and other herbal aromatics.

Recipes

Southern Drum

1 oz. Woodford Reserve rye

¼ oz. simple syrup

2 dashes Woodford Reserve Sassafras & Sorghum bitters

2 oz. Hitachino Nest Espresso Stout

Zest of orange

———————————

In mixing glass, stir rye, simple syrup, and bitters, with ice, for 7 seconds. Strain neat into an Old Fashioned glass. Top with espresso stout and garnish with expressed orange zest.

Try PourTaste's seasonal twist:
For spring or summer, try stirring in ½ oz. of good peach eau du vie in the mixing glass. We suggest eau du vie from Rothman & Winter or Massanez.

Madelena

1 oz. Wisdom & Warter Cream Sherry

5 oz. (or to taste) Urban Family Sour Bog

Pour 1 oz. of cream sherry into glass of choice and top with Sour Bog.

Try PourTaste's seasonal twist:
For a more crisp, spring-like cocktail, try a dry-style sherry like fino or manzanilla in addition to ½ oz. of Luxardo's Bitter Bianco.

Prescription Fizz

1 oz. VSOP armagnac

1 oz. CioCiaro amaro

¼ oz. lemon juice

4 oz. Stiegl Radler

Zest of grapefruit

In shaking tin, combine armagnac, amaro, and lemon, then shake, with ice, for 10 seconds. Strain over fresh ice into an Old Fashioned glass. Top with Stiegl Radler. Garnish with expressed grapefruit zest.

Try PourTaste's seasonal twist:
Substituting an un-aged (clear) armagnac, like that from Delord or Arton, will be right up your alley if you like lighter weight cocktails made with gin or vodka. Also, a dusting of nutmeg on the finished libation will pair wonderfully with the grapefruit.

Gilded Trophy

2 pieces of pineapple (plus extra for garnish)

¾ oz. simple syrup

2 oz. rye whiskey

¾ oz. lemon juice

2 dashes Angostura bitters

Aecht Schlenkerla smoke beer

In shaking tin, muddle pineapple chunks into simple syrup. Add whiskey, lemon juice, and bitters, and shake, with ice, for 10 seconds. Strain over fresh ice and top with smoke beer, to taste. Garnish with pineapple.

> **Try PourTaste's seasonal twist:**
> *Shaking 1 oz. of cream sherry in this libation will be a wonderful autumn delight.*

Ginger Lindsay #2

1-inch disc of cucumber

¾ oz. ginger syrup*

¾ oz. lemon juice

2 oz. London dry gin

Sam Smith Apricot Ale

Cucumber for garnish

_____

In shaking tin, muddle cucumber into ginger syrup. Add lemon juice and gin and shake, with ice, for 10 seconds. Strain over fresh ice and top with Sam Smith Apricot Ale, to taste. Garnish with cucumber.

*INSTRUCTIONS FOR GINGER SYRUP: In saucepan, combine one cup of finely chopped ginger root, one cup of sugar, and 2 cups of water. Bring to boil, stir until sugar is dissolved, then let simmer for 30 minutes. Strain out ginger pieces and enjoy!

Try PourTaste's seasonal twist:
Try topping this off with a watermelon lager or watermelon sour for a poolside cooler.

Sicilian Pour Over

1 oz. Montenegro amaro

2 dashes Fee Brothers cardamom bitters

Gotta Get Up To Get Down Coffee Stout

Zest of orange

_____

In an Old Fashioned glass, combine amaro and cardamom bitters. Top with coffee stout, stir, and garnish with expressed orange zest.

> **Try PourTaste's seasonal twist:**
> _Simply changing out your bitters in this drink will really give you a lot of options. Try molé, chocolate, or a clove-heavy Old Fashioned bitters._

The Paisley

1 oz. Barsol Quebranta pisco

1 oz. ginger syrup (page 10)

¾ oz. lime juice

¼ oz. simple syrup

2 oz. Kasteel Rouge

Mint leaf

In a shaking tin, combine pisco, ginger syrup, lime juice, and simple syrup and shake, with ice, for 10 seconds. Strain neat into a champagne coupe or martini glass. Top with Kasteel Rouge. Garnish with one expressed mint leaf.

Try PourTaste's seasonal twist:
In place of pisco, we suggest substituting mezcal, for something that will offer a bit more "chest hair," as we like to say.

Corcovado

2 oz. Foursquare rum

¾ oz. lime juice

¾ oz. simple syrup

4 oz. Perennial chamomile beer

In shaking tin, combine rum, lime juice, and syrup, and shake, with ice, for 10 seconds. Strain neat and top with chamomile beer, in equal proportion to the cocktail.

Try PourTaste's seasonal twist:
Add 5 dashes of E Harlow magnolia bitters for even more springtime floral notes. Feeling tiki? Try substituting ginger syrup in place of regular simple syrup.

Moonrise Hotel

1 oz. Kronan Swedish Punsch

1 oz. Bonal

¾ oz. lime juice

¼ oz. honey

2 dashes Angostura bitters

3 oz. Ace pineapple cider

_____

In shaking tin, combine Punsch, Bonal, lime juice, honey, and bitters, and shake with ice for 10 seconds. Strain over fresh ice and top with pineapple cider.

Try PourTaste's seasonal twist:
For fall/winter, try topping this off with a good, French-born apple cider.

Tonic Spritzer

1 oz. E Harlow Pristine Tonic

¾ oz. Rothman & Winter Apricot

5–6 oz. Tecate

Shake tonic and apricot liqueur in a shaking tin, with ice, for 6 seconds. Strain neat and top with Tecate to taste.

Try PourTaste's seasonal twist:
We love creme de cassis (black currant liqueur) in this drink, a lot. The deeper notes will be a wonderful pairing for the fall and winter months. Cranberry cordial is also astonishing. Try the one from Clear Creek Distillery.

Jaquiri

2 oz. dark Jamaican or Barbados rum

¾ oz. lime juice

1 barspoon of grapefruit juice

¾ oz. jaggery syrup*

1 barspoon St. Elizabeth Allspice Dram

2 oz. Spiced holiday ale

Lime wheel for garnish

In shaking tin, combine rum, juices, jaggery syrup, and Allspice Dram, and shake with ice for 10 seconds. Strain neat into a glass. Top with a local, seasonal, holiday ale. Garnish with lime wheel.

*INSTRUCTIONS FOR JAGGERY SYRUP: Jaggery, which is an Asian raw sugar, comes in blocks and needs to be broken into smaller pieces. Cut off a piece about the size of a lemon and let melt into 2 cups of simmering water, in saucepan. Ready for use once dissolved.

Try PourTaste's seasonal twist: *Try muddling blackberries in this drink during the summertime!*

Heart of Harlow

1 oz. Nardini grappa

1 oz. papaya syrup*

1 oz. Dansk ginger mead

¾ oz. lemon juice

4 dashes Scrappy's lavender bitters

1 oz. Boulevard Tropical Pale Ale

In shaking tin, combine grappa, syrup, mead, lemon juice, and bitters, and shake with ice for 7 seconds. Strain neat and top with tropical ale.

***INSTRUCTIONS FOR PAPAYA SYRUP:** In saucepan, combine 2 cups chopped papaya, 2 cups water, and 1 cup sugar. Bring to boil and let simmer for 30 minutes. Strain and use.

> **Try PourTaste's seasonal twist:**
> *The addition of muddled pineapple will send this recipe to the moon and back.*

Fancy Tokyo Tippler

2 oz. Gekkeikan Black & Gold sake

½ oz. lemongrass syrup*

2 dashes Regan's orange bitters

Hitachino Nest pilsner

Zest of lemon

_____

In mixing glass, stir sake, lemongrass syrup, and bitters with ice for 7 seconds. Strain neat into champagne coupe. Top with pilsner and garnish with expressed lemon zest.

***INSTRUCTIONS FOR LEMONGRASS SYRUP:** Combine 1 cup of finely chopped lemongrass with 1 cup of water and 1 cup of sugar in a saucepan. Bring to boil then let simmer for 30 minutes, stirring often. Strain and use.

Try PourTaste's seasonal twist:
Instead of stirring, try shaking this recipe with the addition of ¾ oz. of yuzu juice. The lemon-like acidity of yuzu will make for a frothy and light summertime delight.

Porter Cup (à la Jerry Thomas)

1-inch disc of cucumber

½ oz. ginger syrup (page 10)

1 oz. Pierre Ferrand cognac

2–3 oz. St. Peter's Porter

Nutmeg

Zest of lemon

In shaking tin, muddle disc of cucumber into ginger syrup. Add cognac and shake with ice for 8 seconds. Strain over fresh ice into collins glass, top with St. Peter's Porter, and garnish with an expressed lemon zest along with a light dusting of grated nutmeg.

Try PourTaste's seasonal twist:
Topping this cocktail with a pear-based cider instead of the bolder style of Porter will lighten this drink up for spring and summer.

Sunset Kingdom

2 oz. Carpano bianco vermouth

½ oz. lemon juice

½ oz. simple syrup

2 dashes Regan's orange bitters

2 oz. Pale ale of choice

_____

In shaking tin, combine vermouth, lemon juice, syrup, and bitters, and shake with ice for 6 seconds. Strain neat and top with pale ale of choice.

Try PourTaste's seasonal twist:
The addition of ½ oz. of good apricot or peach liqueur will elevate this simple pleasure to a serious summer delight.

Fernet & Falernum

1 oz. Florio fernet

1 oz. lime juice

1 oz. Luxardo orgeat

4 oz. Hitachino Nest Ginger Brew

In shaking tin, combine fernet, lime juice, and orgeat, and shake with ice for 7 seconds. Strain neat and top with ginger beer.

Try PourTaste's seasonal twist:
Falernum is a classic island mix based off ginger, almond, and lime, though other baking spices are used as well. A grating of nutmeg or cinnamon in this drink will amplify its Caribbean inspiration.

Herringbone

1 ½ oz. Amargo Vallet Angostura

1 oz. Benedictine

1 oz. jaggery syrup (page 22)

¾ oz. lemon juice

2 oz. extra stout of choice

_____

In shaking tin, combine Amargo, Benedictine, syrup, and lemon juice, and shake with ice for 10 seconds. Strain over fresh ice, top with a bitter, extra stout, and enjoy.

> **Try PourTaste's seasonal twist:**
> _This is a fairly low-alcohol cocktail. Try adding ¾ oz. of whiskey of choice to add body and depth._

Bitter Williams

1 ½ oz. carrot juice

¾ oz. lime juice

1 oz. Belle de Brillet pear brandy

1 oz. Salers aperitif

4 dashes Bitter Truth celery bitters

2 oz. Kolsch-style beer

Pear slices, for garnish

In shaking tin, combine juices, pear brandy, Salers, and bitters, and shake with ice for 7 seconds. Strain over fresh ice, top with a Kolsch-style beer and garnish with pear slices.

Try PourTaste's seasonal twist:
We liked adding gin to this libation. 1 oz. of a trusted London dry will add a crisp, epicurean edge to this. Muddling a disc of cucumber will enhance this in the summertime as well.

Calico Tea

1 ½ oz. Calvados

¾ oz. lemon juice

¾ oz. sage-black tea syrup*

2 dashes Angostura bitters

2 oz. Barleywine-style ale

_____

In shaking tin, combine calvados, lemon juice, syrup, and bitters, and shake with ice for 10 seconds. Strain over fresh ice and top with barleywine-style ale.

***INSTRUCTIONS FOR SAGE-BLACK TEA SYRUP:** In saucepan, combine 1 cup water, 1 cup sugar, ¼ cup loose leaf black tea, and ¼ cup finely chopped sage. Bring to boil then let simmer for 30 minutes, stirring often. Strain and use.

> **Try PourTaste's seasonal twist:**
> *Add ½ oz. of overproof Demerara or Barbados rum for the late summer and early fall.*

The Gulfside of Things

½ **nectarine, pitted**

¼ **oz. simple syrup**

1 **oz. Nardini Mandorla grappa**

Miller High Life

In shaking tin, muddle nectarine into simple syrup. Add grappa and shake with ice for 6 seconds. Strain neat into pint glass and top with High Life.

Try PourTaste's seasonal twist:
Apricot brandy also works really well in this drink.

Cheekwood Swizzle

1 oz. Pistachio-infused green Chartreuse*

1 oz. lime juice

½ oz. simple syrup

1 oz. coconut milk

2 oz. Helles-style lager

Mint leaf

_____

In shaking tin, combine infused Chartreuse, lime juice, simple syrup, and coconut milk, and shake with ice for 7 seconds. Strain over fresh ice and top with helles-style lager. Garnish with expressed mint.

*INSTRUCTIONS FOR PISTACHIO-INFUSED GREEN CHARTREUSE: In mason jar of choice, fill half full with shelled, salted pistachios. Fill jar with green Chartreuse. Seal, shake, and let sit at least one week. Strain and use.

Try PourTaste's seasonal twist:
Feeling multi-cultural? Try muddling a handful of cilantro in this for a strangely Thai-like cocktail.

Anglo Saxon Punch

2 oz. Dansk hopped mead

½ oz. lime juice

½ oz. Luxardo orgeat

1 barspoon of Wray & Nephew rum

2 oz. Schneider Weisse Hopfenweisse

Lime wheel, for garnish

_____

In shaking tin, combine mead, lime juice, and orgeat, and shake with ice for 7 seconds. Strain neat into a rum-rinsed glass and top with Schneider Weisse. Garnish with lime wheel.

Try PourTaste's seasonal twist:
Try making this with white whiskey in place of the mead. It will yield some wonderful aromatics for this cocktail.

Thatcher's Revenge

6–8 oz. Scotch-style ale

¾ oz. persimmon-brown sugar syrup*

4 dashes chai tea tincture**

In glass of choice, pour ale and add syrup and bitters. Stir and enjoy!

***INSTRUCTIONS FOR PERSIMMON-BROWN SUGAR SYRUP:** In saucepan, combine 1 cup water, 1 cup brown sugar, and 1 cup diced persimmon. Bring mixture to a boil then let simmer for 30 minutes. Strain and use.

*****INSTRUCTIONS FOR CHAI TEA TINCTURE:** Fill an 8 oz. mason jar half full with loose leaf chai tea. Fill the jar with brandy, seal, and let sit for at least 2 weeks. Strain and transfer to a dropper bottle.

Try PourTaste's seasonal twist:
For a bit more of a winter kick, try adding 1 ½ oz. of Scotch. The same amount dark Jamaican rum will pull this libation in a wonderful tiki direction as well.

Czech, Please

Pilsner Urquell

1 oz. bitter orange syrup*

_____

Pour Pilsner Urquell into glass of choice and add one ounce of bitter orange syrup. Stir and enjoy.

*INSTRUCTIONS FOR BITTER ORANGE SYRUP: Add 1 cup water, 1 cup sugar, and ½ cup dried, bitter orange peel in saucepan. Bring to boil then let simmer for 30 minutes. Stir often, strain, and use.

Try PourTaste's seasonal twist:
The addition of ½ oz. of peach or apricot brandy will be an amazing springtime addition.

The Rosenthal

1 lime

¾ oz. simple syrup

2 oz. cachaca

5 oz. Sierra Nevada Bigfoot barleywine-style ale

Cut your lime in half, then into quarters. In shaking tin, muddle two pieces of lime into simple syrup. Add cachaca and shake, with ice, for 10 seconds. Strain and top with Bigfoot barleywine.

Try PourTaste's seasonal twist:
Muddling mint into this cocktail might be one of our favorite additions. Sometimes simple is best.

Some Sort of Mule

1 ½ oz. green tea-infused vodka*

¾ oz. lime juice

¾ oz. ginger syrup (page 10)

½ oz. pear brandy

2–4 oz. Beerlao (or to taste)

_____

In shaking tin, combine vodka, lime juice, ginger syrup, and pear brandy, and shake with ice for 10 seconds. Strain over fresh ice and top with Beerlao.

*INSTRUCTIONS FOR GREEN TEA INFUSED VODKA: In a one-quart mason jar, add ¼ cup loose leaf green tea. Fill with vodka of choice. Seal, shake, and let sit for 2 weeks. Strain and use.

> **Try PourTaste's seasonal twist:**
> _For fall/winter, infuse the vodka with a black tea of choice and substitute creme de cassis (black currant liqueur) instead of pear._

Magnolia Shandy

La Chouffe Belgian Ale

E Harlow magnolia bitters

Zest of lemon

_____

Pour La Chouffe into glass of choice. Add 6 dashes of E Harlow magnolia bitters and stir. Garnish with expressed lemon zest.

Try PourTaste's seasonal twist:
Experiment with the Belgian beer component. Try this recipe with a dubbel, triple, or even a quad style.

Preservationist

1 ½ oz. Batavia Arrack

1 oz. Aperol

¾ oz. lime juice

¾ oz. ginger syrup (page 10)

1 barspoon coconut cream

2 oz. Coors

Lime wheel

In shaking tin, combine Batavia, Aperol, lime juice, ginger syrup, and coconut cream, and shake vigorously for 10 seconds. Strain over fresh ice and top with Coors. Garnish with a lime wheel.

Try PourTaste's seasonal twist:
Using mezcal in place of Batavia is a wonderful next step for this cocktail.

Athena

1 ½ oz. gin

1 oz. Carpano Bianco vermouth

1 oz. Giffard pamplemousse rośe

2 dashes Regan's orange bitters

Light lager of choice

Zest of lemon

_____

In mixing glass, stir gin, vermouth, bitters, and Giffard, with ice for 10 seconds. Strain neat into a champagne coupe. Top with an American light lager of choice and garnish with expressed lemon zest.

Try PourTaste's seasonal twist:
If you're a fan of grapefruit, you can top this off with the grapefruit-forward Stiegl Radler instead. If you're wanting more depth, try their lemon radler.

Society Islands Fizz

¾ oz. Benedictine

¾ oz. Pierre Ferrand Dry Curacao

6–8 oz. Kolsch-style beer

Mint

Shake Benedictine and curaçao in shaking tin, with ice, for 7 seconds. Strain over ice into tiki mug and top with Kolsch-style beer. Garnish with mint.

Try PourTaste's seasonal twist:
The fall season will call for the addition of 1 oz. of a dark amaro, like Montenegro, CioCiaro, or Averna.

Plantation Punch

2 oz. Brandy

1 oz. Cappelletti

½ oz. Old Man guava berry liqueur

2 oz. Wheat beer of choice

In mixing glass, combine brandy, Cappelletti, and guava berry liqueur, and stir with ice for 10 seconds. Strain neat into an Old Fashioned glass and top with wheat-style beer, to taste.

Try PourTaste's seasonal twist:
Instead of brandy, try bourbon, then top this off with an IPA.

Vicksburg & Liberty

1 oz. Gifford banana liqueur

3 oz. Champagne

3 oz. Guinness

In glass of choice, pour liqueur, then Champagne. Pour Guinness into mixture, stir, and enjoy.

Try PourTaste's seasonal twist:
The experiment to run here is changing out the fruit liqueurs. We think blackberry would be a great addition during the fall and winter seasons.

Nano Classic

Trip in the Woods barrel-aged ginger beer

Wray & Nephew white overproof rum

Lime wedge

_____

Rinse glass with rum, pour in barrel-aged ginger beer, and add a squeeze of lime juice.

Try PourTaste's seasonal twist:
The addition of cardamom bitters take this in a wonderful, earthy direction.

Blood Red & By the Minute

1 oz. Mezcal

1 oz. Campari

1 oz. Sweet vermouth

1 oz. IPA of choice

In mixing glass, stir mezcal, Campari, and sweet vermouth, with ice for 10 seconds. Strain neat and top with an IPA of choice.

Try PourTaste's seasonal twist:
Try topping this with a sour-style beer. Watermelon Gose is starting to hit the market, or even a peach-based sour.

The Drop

Stiegl Radler

1 oz. Luxardo Maraschino

In glass of choice, pour Radler, then pour in maraschino. Give it a quick stir, and enjoy.

Try PourTaste's seasonal twist:
Try stirring in 1 oz. of gin to make this more of a "cocktail."

Oatmeal Stout Old Fashioned

2 dashes Fee Brothers black walnut bitters

Sam Smith Oatmeal Stout

Zest of orange

Pour stout into glass, then stir in black walnut bitters. Garnish with expressed orange zest.

Try PourTaste's seasonal twist: *Rinse the glass with overproof Demerara or Barbados rum for aromatics.*

Frozen Brandy Crusta

2 oz. Pierre Ferrand 1840 cognac

¾ oz. Pierre Ferrand Dry Curacao

½ oz. lemon juice

½ oz. simple syrup

2 dashes Angostura bitters

2 cups ice

4 oz. Hefeweizen-style beer

In a blender, combine cognac, curacao, lemon juice, simple syrup, and bitters, and blend with 2 cups ice until smooth. Pour neat into glass of choice and top with Hefeweizen-style beer.

Try PourTaste's seasonal twist:
For a summertime delight, add ½ oz. of Giffard banana liqueur. It will pair extremely well with the Hefeweizen.

Brasserie

1 oz. VSOP cognac

¼ oz. Belle de Brillet pear brandy

½ oz. lemon juice

¼ oz. simple syrup

St. Fullien Saison

Slice of pear

_____

In shaking tin, combine cognac, pear brandy, lemon juice, and simple syrup, and shake with ice for 10 seconds. Strain over fresh ice into an Old Fashioned glass. Top with St. Fullien Saison. Garnish with pear slice.

> **Try PourTaste's seasonal twist:**
> *The addition of celery bitters adds a wonderful complexity to this cocktail.*

Holiness

1 oz. dark-style amaro

¾ oz. lemon juice

½ oz. Giffard banana liqueur

4 oz. Kagua Blanc

In shaking tin, combine amaro, lemon juice, and banana liqueur, and shake with ice for 7 seconds. Strain over fresh ice and top with Kagua Blanc.

Try PourTaste's seasonal twist:
Pear, peach, or apricot brandies are the items to experiment with here, in place of the banana.

Mississippi Porter Punch

¾ oz. bourbon

¾ oz. VSOP cognac

¾ oz. dark Jamaican or
   Barbados rum

2 dashes Angostura bitters

1 oz. Sam Smith Taddy
   Porter

Zest of orange

In a mixing glass, stir
bourbon, cognac, rum,
and bitters, with ice for 15
seconds. Strain neat into an
Old Fashioned glass and top
with Sam Smith Taddy Porter.
Garnish with expressed
orange zest.

**Try PourTaste's
seasonal twist:**
*For a fall libation, try
infusing your bourbon with
loose leaf earl grey tea.
Also, ½ oz. of cream sherry
stirred in is a very upscale
addition.*

Cusco Sour

1 ½ oz. pisco

¾ oz. lemon juice

½ oz. simple syrup

Whites of one egg

**Southern Grist coconut-
     pineapple beer**

_____

In shaking tin, combine pisco, lemon juice, simple syrup, and egg white, and shake vigorously, with ice, for 15 seconds, in order to froth the whites of the egg. Strain neat into champagne coupe and top with Southern Grist coconut-pineapple beer to taste.

**Try PourTaste's
seasonal twist:**
_For the holidays, try
topping this with a
cranberry ale instead!_

Seersucker

4 medium-size cubes of watermelon

½ oz. simple syrup

1 oz. lime juice

Abita Strawberry Lager

Mint leaf

In shaking tin, muddle watermelon into simple syrup. Add lime juice and shake for 5 seconds. Strain neat into champagne coupe and top with strawberry lager. Garnish with an expressed mint leaf.

Try PourTaste's seasonal twist:
Adding 1 oz. of a dry style sherry, like fino, elevates this drink into a serious work of art.

Imperial Drag

1 oz. Appleton Estate VX rum

4 dashes Fee Brothers Old Fashioned bitters

¾ oz. Massanez Creme de Cassis

Turtle Anarchy Portly Stout

Zest of orange

In a mixing glass, stir rum, bitters, and creme de cassis, with ice, for 10 seconds. Strain neat into an Old Fashioned glass. Fill remainder of glass with Turtle Anarchy Portly Stout. Garnish with expressed orange zest.

> **Try PourTaste's seasonal twist:**
> *Try substituting a raspberry or cranberry liqueur instead of cassis.*

The Manchester Star

1 oz. Lairds 100 proof Applejack

1 oz. ruby port

2 dashes Angostura bitters

4 oz. Manchester Star English Ale

Zest of orange

In mixing glass, stir apple brandy, port, and bitters, with ice for 10 seconds. Strain neat and top with Manchester Star English Ale. Garnish with expressed orange zest.

Try PourTaste's seasonal twist:
For a bit more complexity, try sweet vermouth instead of port.

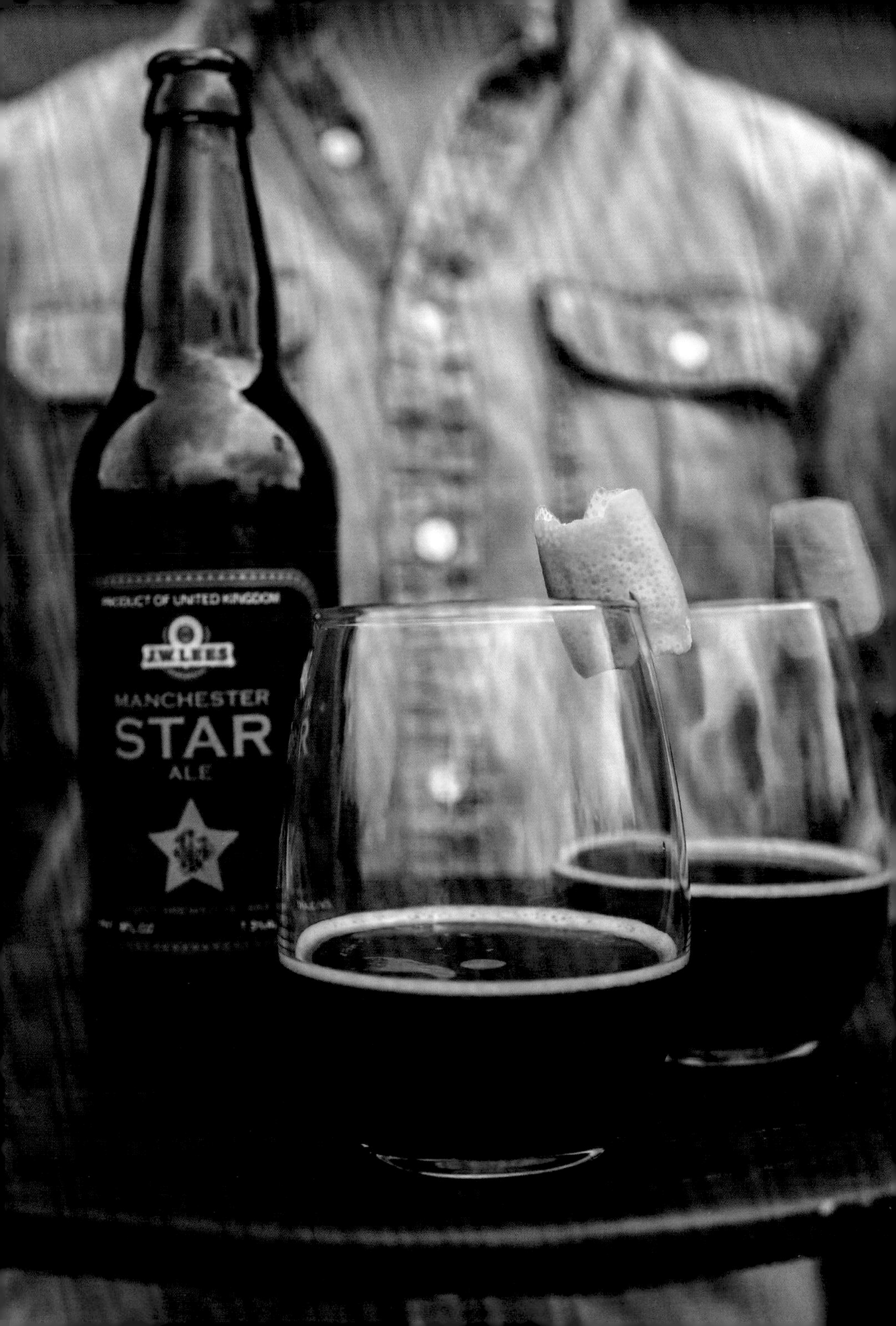
PRODUCT OF UNITED KINGDOM
J.W.LEES
MANCHESTER
STAR
ALE

The Sisterhood

1 ½ oz. blanco tequila

¾ oz. lime juice

½ oz. simple syrup

Freshly grated cinnamon

4 oz. Stiegl Radler

In shaking tin, combine tequila, lime juice, syrup, and a quick, fresh grating of cinnamon and shake, with ice, for 10 seconds. Strain over fresh ice and top with Stiegl Radler.

Try PourTaste's seasonal twist:
This recipe works extremely well with gin, mezcal, or vodka in place of the tequila.

Printers Alley Punch

1-inch disc of cucumber

1 oz. quince syrup*

2 oz. Pimm's

1 oz. London dry gin

¾ oz. lemon juice

4 drops black tea tincture**

2 oz. Dark English porter of choice

_____

In shaking tin, muddle cucumber into quince syrup. Add Pimms, gin, lemon juice, and tincture and shake, with ice, for 10 seconds. Strain over fresh ice and top with English Porter.

***INSTRUCTIONS FOR QUINCE SYRUP:** In saucepan, combine 1 cup water, 1 cup sugar, and 1 cup quince paste. Bring to a boil then let simmer for 30 minutes. Stir often, then strain using a fine mesh strainer and use.

****INSTRUCTIONS FOR BLACK TEA TINCTURE:** Fill an 8 oz. mason jar half full with loose leaf black tea of choice. Fill the jar with brandy, seal, and let sit for at least 2 weeks. Strain and transfer to a dropper bottle.

> **Try PourTaste's seasonal twist:**
> _Try substituting peach brandy for the quince syrup, and add cardamom bitters!_

Tennessee Frisco

1 ½ oz. bourbon

1 oz. Benedictine

¾ oz. lemon juice

¼ oz. simple syrup

2 dashes Angostura bitters

Blackberry Farm Saison

Zest of lemon

_____

In shaking tin, combine bourbon, Benedictine, lemon juice, simple syrup, and bitters, and shake with ice for 10 seconds. Strain neat into a champagne coupe and top with Blackberry Farm Saison. Garnish with expressed lemon zest.

Try PourTaste's seasonal twist:
Try rinsing the glass with absinthe. It's not for everyone but the aromatics are delightful with a saison.

Local Church

1 ½ oz. Red Breast Irish Whiskey

½ oz. Benedictine

¼ oz. Massanez Creme de Cassis

2 dashes Angostura bitters

5 drops black pepper tincture*

2 oz. Irish Red Ale

Zest of orange

_____

Combine whiskey, Benedictine, creme de cassis, bitters, and tincture in mixing glass and stir, with ice, for 10 seconds. Strain neat and top with Irish, red-style ale. Garnish with expressed orange zest.

*INSTRUCTIONS FOR BLACK PEPPER TINCTURE: In small mason jar, let equal parts whole black pepper and brandy sit for at least two weeks, shaking often. Strain and transfer to dropper bottle.

> Try PourTaste's seasonal twist: Topping this cocktail with stout instead of red ale was a smooth transition and a logical next step.

Boneset & Spruce

**1 oz. dark Jamaican or
Barbados rum**

1 oz. VSOP cognac

¾ oz. lemon juice

¾ oz. molasses

**2 oz. Poor Richard's Tavern
Spruce Ale**

Mint

_____

In shaking tin, combine rum, cognac, lemon juice, and molasses, and shake with ice for 10 seconds. Strain over fresh ice and top with spruce ale. Garnish with expressed mint thicket.

> **Try PourTaste's
> seasonal twist:**
> _If you can't find spruce ale, try adding ¼ oz. of Douglas Fir liqueur and topping this with a wheat beer. Also, you can easily forgo the alpine element and top this with a French-born unfiltered cider. It's amazing._

Centennial

Zest of lemon

Zest of orange

¾ oz. Rivulet pecan liqueur

2 oz. Chateau Arton armagnac

4 oz. Lazy Magnolia Southern Pecan ale

_____

Cut a strip of both orange and lemon rind, about the size of an average band-aid. In an Old Fashioned glass, muddle the two pieces of zest and bitters into Rivulet. Add armagnac and stir with ice for 6 seconds. Top with Lazy Magnolia pecan ale.

Try PourTaste's seasonal twist:
Instead of armagnac, try making this Old Fashioned-like drink with a dark Barbados rum instead.

Index

in Centennial, 100
Perennial chamomile beer
  in Corcovado, 16
Persimmon-Brown Sugar Syrup, 46
  in Thatcher's Revenge, 46
Pierre Ferrand cognac
  in Frozen Brandy Crusta, 74
  in Porter Cup (à la Jerry Thomas),
    28
Pierre Ferrand Dry Curacao
  in Frozen Brandy Crusta, 74
  in Society Islands Fizz, 60
Pilsner Urquell
  in Czech, Please, 48
pilsners
  in Fancy Tokyo Tippler, 26
Pimm's
  in Printers Alley Punch, 92
Pimm's Cup, xv
pineapple
  in Gilded Trophy, 8
  in Heart of Harlow, 24
pisco, xxii
  in Cusco Sour, 82
  in The Paisley, 14
Pistachio-Infused Green Chartreuse
  in Cheekwood Swizzle, 42
Plantation Punch, 62
Poor Richard's Tavern Spruce Ale
  in Boneset & Spruce, 98
port
  in The Manchester Star, 88
Porter Cup, xv
Porter Cup (à la Jerry Thomas), 28
porters, xv
  in Mississippi Porter Punch, 80
  in Porter Cup (à la Jerry Thomas),
    28
  in Printers Alley Punch, 92
Prescription Fizz, 6

Preservationist, 56
Printers Alley Punch, 92
punch, xiv
punsch, xxii
  in Moonrise Hotel, 18
Purl, xv
Purl Royale, xv

Q
Quince Syrup, 92
  in Printers Alley Punch, 92

R
radler, xiii, xvi
raspberry liqueur
  in Imperial Drag, 86
red ale
  in Local Church, 96
Red Breast Irish Whiskey
  in Local Church, 96
Regan's orange bitters
  in Athena, 58
  in Fancy Tokyo Tippler, 26
  in Sunset Kingdom, 30
rinsing, xix
Rivulet pecan liqueur
  in Centennial, 100
rośe
  in Athena, 58
Rosenthal, The, 50
Rothman & Winter Apricot
  in Tonic Spritzer, 20
Rothman & Winter eau du vie
  in Southern Drum, 2
ruby port
  in The Manchester Star, 88
rum
  in Anglo Saxon Punch, 44
  in Boneset & Spruce, 98
  in Calico Tea, 38
  in Centennial, 100

About the Authors

Jon and Lindsay Yeager are the creators of the Nashville based cocktail creative PourTaste. Since their marriage in 2011, the Yeagers have been consulting full time for restaurants, hotels, and bars alongside their work with festivals, retail shops, and brands. They are the creators of E Harlow Pristine Tonic and E Harlow Magnolia Bitters and are also the founders of the annual Nashville Cocktail Festival. In addition to these projects, their video series and podcast highlight their desire for education both inside the industry and out. Their "cocktail creative" brings brands and artisans together to push forward the art and craft of the cocktail movement.